POST-DISASTER NEEDS ASSESSMENT

SIMULATION EXERCISE HANDBOOK

SEPTEMBER 2024

ADB

ASIAN DEVELOPMENT BANK

Contents

Typhoon Haiyan (Yolanda) Damage and Rehabilitation (page iii–iv)
Houses destroyed by Typhoon Haiyan in Palo, Leyte (photo by ADB).

Tables, Figures, and Boxes

TABLES

FIGURES

BOXES

Acknowledgments

The *Handbook on Post-Disaster Needs Assessment—Simulation Exercise* was prepared by the Climate Change, Resilience, and Environment Cluster (CCRE)—Disaster Risk Management of the Climate Change and Sustainable Development Department of the Asian Development Bank (ADB). The Asian Disaster Preparedness Center (ADPC) provided technical guidance in the preparation of this handbook.

The purpose of the handbook is to provide ADB staff a reference in conducting a simulation exercise on the Post-Disaster Needs Assessment (PDNA) methodology, particularly on the role of ADB. This handbook complements the Post-Disaster Needs Assessment Overview for ADB staff published by ADB in 2021.

The publication benefited from peer review of the CCRE Disaster Risk Management under its unit head Alexandra Galperin. Maria Anna Orquiza, senior disaster risk management officer, CCRE, provided guidance in the development of the publication with technical inputs from Sifayet Mohammad Ullah, disaster risk management specialist, CCRE. The handbook was developed based on the PDNA Introductory Course conducted in August 2023 for staff of the ADB resident missions in Bangladesh, Nepal, and Sri Lanka. Steven Goldfinch, senior disaster risk management specialist, CRRE, provided leadership in the development and delivery of the PDNA Introductory Course with support from Maria Anna Orquiza and Sifayet Mohammad Ullah.

Thitiphon Sinsupan, PDNA specialist, ADPC, and Mona Chhabra Anand, resilient recovery specialist, ADPC, developed the technical publication. Rocilyn Locsin Laccay (ADB consultant) provided graphics and layout services.

Abbreviations

ADB	Asian Development Bank
DMC	developing member country
PDNA	post-disaster needs assessment
km	kilometer

Typhoon Haiyan (Yolanda) Damage and Rehabilitation.
View from a window of a destroyed house in Barangay 67, Tacloban, Leyte (photo by ADB).

About the Handbook

BACKGROUND

Disasters have posed significant challenges to development investments the world over, seen in the upward trend in the loss of life and property in the past few decades. Extreme climate events have exacerbated this trend. A scientific estimate of disaster (climate-induced as well as geophysical) effects is crucial for planning the replacement of impacted assets, building back better, and becoming more resilient in the face of future shocks. According to the 2021 Disaster and Emergency Assistance Policy[1] of the Asian Development Bank (ADB), disasters have resulted in the loss of 676,924 lives in ADB's developing member countries (DMCs) and affected 2.31 billion people from 2004 to 2020. This accounted for 62% of disaster-related fatalities globally. Reported direct physical damage in DMCs totaled $696 billion over the same period, with an average direct physical damage of $112 million per day.

ADB is committed to poverty reduction and sustainable development through a range of investments targeted at strengthening disaster resilience in DMCs. ADB's 2021 Disaster and Emergency Assistance Policy also emphasizes that emergency assistance projects should be based on the findings of post-disaster needs assessment (PDNA), including evidence of significant economic dislocation and the need to address immediate recovery needs and/or expedite the preparation of regular projects. A PDNA exercise is typically led by the government and undertaken in collaboration with development partners, providing consolidated information on the physical, economic, and human impacts of a disaster. The assessment serves as a critical point of reference for coordinated action by various stakeholders for post-disaster recovery.

To deepen the understanding of its staff on various aspects of PDNA, ADB engaged the Asian Disaster Preparedness Center to enhance its existing training materials with the inclusion of a simulation exercise detailing the various stages, opportunities, and challenges of the PDNA process.

DEVELOPMENT OF THE HANDBOOK

This handbook has been developed based on the experience of pilot training along with simulation exercises conducted for ADB's Sri Lanka Resident Mission in Colombo on 24–25 August, and Bangladesh Resident Mission and Nepal Resident Mission in Dhaka on 28–29 August 2023. The participants included technical and operational staff from the three resident missions with varying degrees of experience and understanding of the PDNA process. The sessions were instrumental in shaping the final format of the 2-day training module presented in this handbook.

This handbook is complementary to PDNA training materials and publications developed by ADB. The purpose of the handbook is thus to facilitate future internal training by enabling staff to build their capacity in undertaking PDNA and deepen their understanding of the methodology through simulation exercises.

INTENDED AUDIENCE OF THE HANDBOOK

The handbook is targeted at staff of ADB resident missions involved in PDNAs, who are expected to be equipped with knowledge to help their colleagues understand the nuances of the exercise and leverage their support at various stages of the process in the future, as required.

---

[1] Asian Development Bank. 2021. Revised Disaster and Emergency Assistance Policy (R-Paper). September 2021.

SUGGESTED TRAINING SCHEDULE

The broad flow of the training with simulation exercise is outlined in Box 1.

Box 1: Day 1. Proposed Program on Post-Disaster Needs Assessment Introductory Training

Time	Session
DAY 1	
8:30–9:00 a.m.	**Registration**
9:00–9:20 a.m.	**Opening and Stage Setting**
9:20–10:00 a.m.	**PDNA Fundamentals** • Introduction to PDNA • ADB and PDNA
10:00–10:30 a.m.	**Break with class photo**
10:30–11:30 a.m.	**PDNA Fundamentals** • The PDNA Methodology » Context Analysis » Disaster Effects
11:30 a.m.–12:30 p.m.	**PDNA Fundamentals** • The PDNA Methodology » Disaster Impacts
12:30–1:30 p.m.	**Lunch**
1:30–2:30 p.m.	**Sector Discussion with Cross-Cutting and Exercises**
2:30–3:30 p.m.	**PDNA Fundamentals** • The PDNA Methodology: » Recovery Needs and Priorities
3:00–3:30 p.m.	**Break**
3:30–4:15 p.m.	**PDNA Fundamentals** • The PDNA Methodology: » Recovery Strategy
4:15–4:30 p.m.	**Wrap-up and Reminders for Day 2**
DAY 2	
9:00 a.m.–3:30 p.m.	**Simulation Exercise**
3:30–4:30 p.m.	**Debriefing and Closing**

ADB = Asian Development Bank, PDNA = post-disaster needs assessment.
Source: Asian Development Bank (Climate Change and Sustainable Development Department).

The PDNA Introductory Training is a 2-day event. On the first day, participants learn about the fundamentals of PDNA, including the process, methodology, and role of ADB in PDNAs. The second day focuses on the practical application of PDNA through a simulation exercise.

OPENING AND PRELIMINARIES

This session begins with welcome remarks by the ADB resident mission country director or representative, followed by introduction of the training team and participants. The session covers training objectives and housekeeping reminders.

TRAINING SESSIONS

The various sessions of the training are designed to cover the basics of PDNA over 2 days. A brief outline of the six sessions for Day 1 is presented in Figure 1 while the full deck of slides for each session is available on request.

Figure 1: Opening and Preliminaries

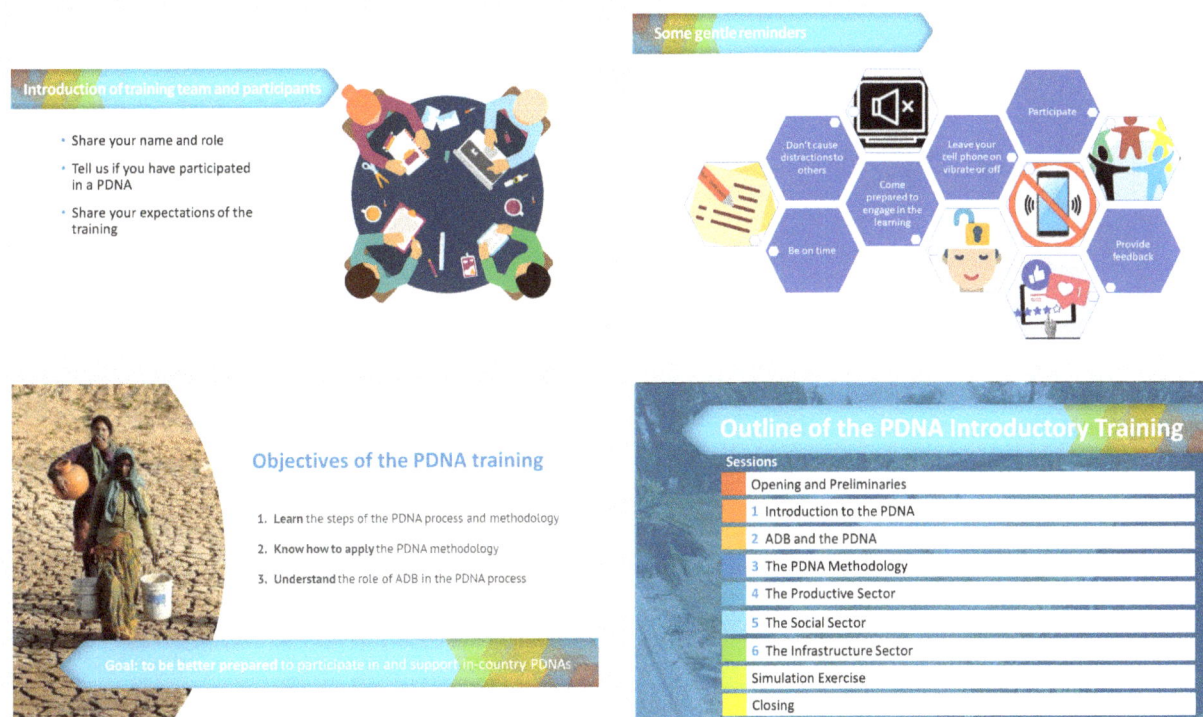

ADB = Asian Development Bank, PDNA = post-disaster needs assessment.
Source: Asian Development Bank (Climate Change and Sustainable Development Department).

1   Session 1: Introduction to the Post-Disaster Needs Assessment

This session presents an overview of PDNA, covering its evolution, purpose, and framework. It includes background information on the PDNA, guidelines, key actors, implementation process, coordination structure, sectors, cross-cutting issues, and deliverables. Additionally, the session discusses requirements and limitations of PDNA (Figure 2).

Figure 2: Coverage of Session 1—Introduction to Post-Disaster Needs Assessment

PDNA = post-disaster needs assessment.
Source: Asian Development Bank (Climate Change and Sustainable Development Department).

2 Session 2: ADB and the Post-Disaster Needs Assessment

The objective of this session is to examine the role of ADB in PDNA. The session provides information about ADB's participation in PDNAs, the importance of PDNAs to ADB, ADB's role in PDNA and the types of support it provides, and the key steps in preparing for a PDNA (Figure 3).

Figure 3: Coverage of Session 2—The Role of ADB in Post-Disaster Needs Assessment

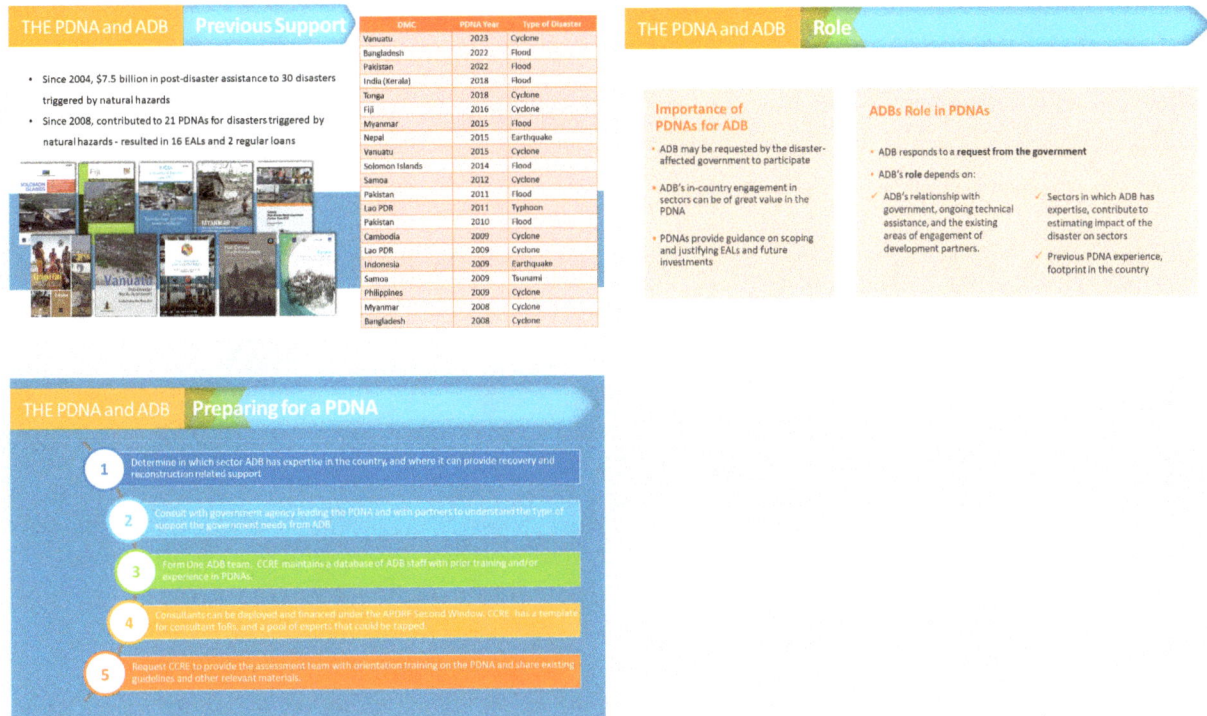

THE PDNA and ADB — Previous Support

- Since 2004, $7.5 billion in post-disaster assistance to 30 disasters triggered by natural hazards
- Since 2008, contributed to 21 PDNAs for disasters triggered by natural hazards - resulted in 16 EALs and 2 regular loans

DMC	PDNA Year	Type of Disaster
Vanuatu	2023	Cyclone
Bangladesh	2022	Flood
Pakistan	2022	Flood
India (Kerala)	2018	Flood
Tonga	2018	Cyclone
Fiji	2016	Cyclone
Myanmar	2015	Flood
Nepal	2015	Earthquake
Vanuatu	2015	Cyclone
Solomon Islands	2014	Flood
Samoa	2012	Cyclone
Pakistan	2011	Flood
Lao PDR	2011	Typhoon
Pakistan	2010	Flood
Cambodia	2009	Cyclone
Lao PDR	2009	Cyclone
Indonesia	2009	Earthquake
Samoa	2009	Tsunami
Philippines	2009	Cyclone
Myanmar	2008	Cyclone
Bangladesh	2008	Cyclone

THE PDNA and ADB — Role

Importance of PDNAs for ADB
- ADB may be requested by the disaster-affected government to participate
- ADB's in-country engagement in sectors can be of great value in the PDNA
- PDNAs provide guidance on scoping and justifying EALs and future investments

ADBs Role in PDNAs
- ADB responds to a request from the government
- ADB's role depends on:
  - ADB's relationship with government, ongoing technical assistance, and the existing areas of engagement of development partners.
  - Sectors in which ADB has expertise, contribute to estimating impact of the disaster on sectors
  - Previous PDNA experience, footprint in the country

THE PDNA and ADB — Preparing for a PDNA

1. Determine in which sector ADB has expertise in the country, and where it can provide recovery and reconstruction related support
2. Consult with government agency leading the PDNA and with partners to understand the type of support the government needs from ADB
3. Form the ADB team. CCRE maintains a database of ADB staff with prior training and/or experience in PDNAs.
4. Consultants can be deployed and financed under the APDRF Second Window. CCRE has a template for consultant ToRs, and a pool of experts that could be tapped.
5. Request CCRE to provide the assessment team with orientation training on the PDNA and share existing guidelines and other relevant materials.

ADB = Asian Development Bank, PDNA = post-disaster needs assessment.
Source: Asian Development Bank (Climate Change and Sustainable Development Department).

3   Session 3: The Post-Disaster Needs Assessment Methodology

The objective of this session is to explain the PDNA process and its methodology. The session introduces five key elements of the PDNA, namely, context analysis, disaster effects, disaster impacts, recovery needs, and recovery strategy (Figure 4).

Figure 4: Coverage of Session 3—The Post-Disaster Needs Assessment Methodology

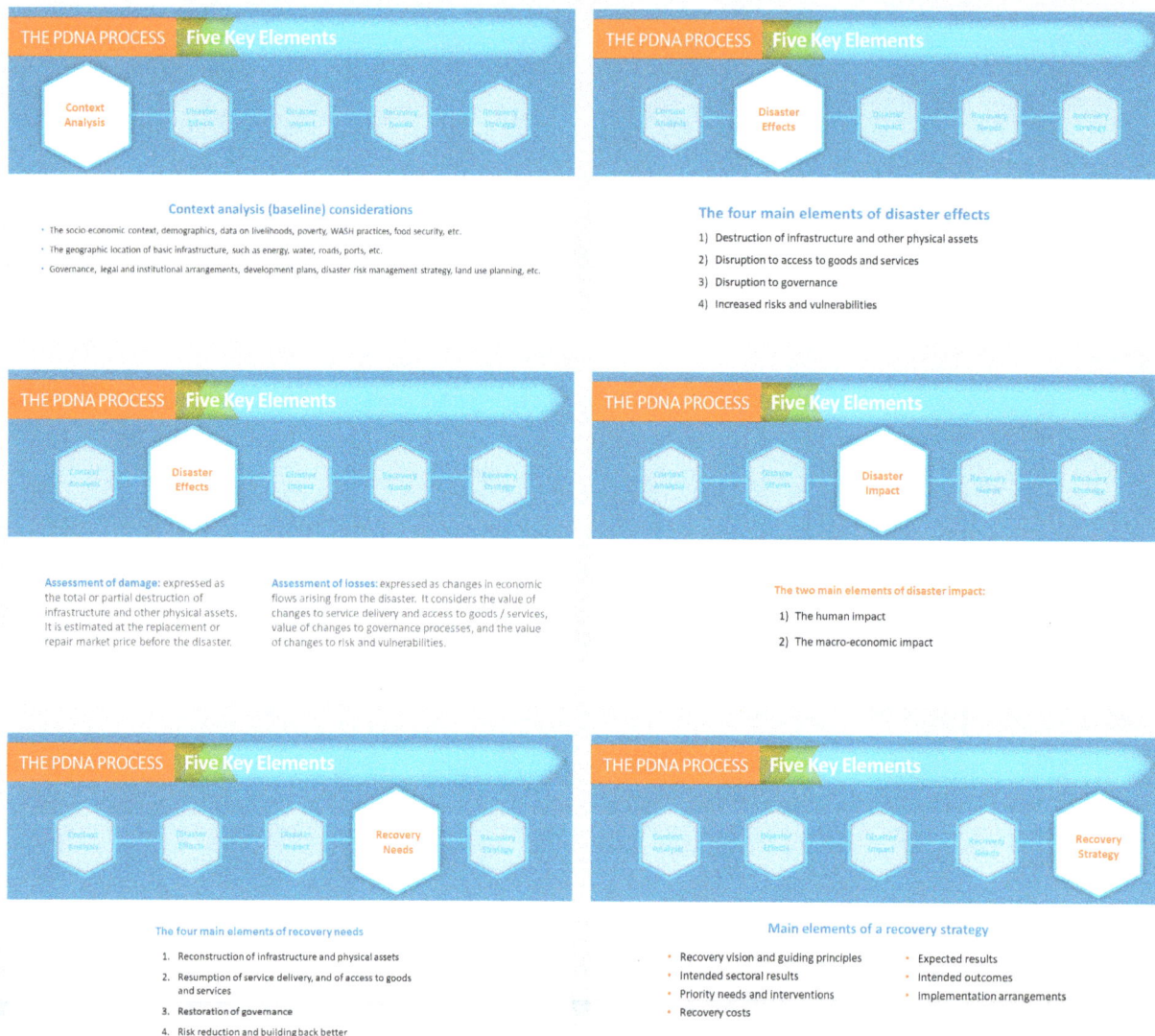

Context analysis (baseline) considerations

- The socio-economic context, demographics, data on livelihoods, poverty, WASH practices, food security, etc.
- The geographic location of basic infrastructure, such as energy, water, roads, ports, etc.
- Governance, legal and institutional arrangements, development plans, disaster risk management strategy, land use planning, etc.

The four main elements of disaster effects

1) Destruction of infrastructure and other physical assets
2) Disruption to access to goods and services
3) Disruption to governance
4) Increased risks and vulnerabilities

Assessment of damage: expressed as the total or partial destruction of infrastructure and other physical assets. It is estimated at the replacement or repair market price before the disaster.

Assessment of losses: expressed as changes in economic flows arising from the disaster. It considers the value of changes to service delivery and access to goods / services, value of changes to governance processes, and the value of changes to risk and vulnerabilities.

The two main elements of disaster impact:

1) The human impact
2) The macro-economic impact

The four main elements of recovery needs

1. Reconstruction of infrastructure and physical assets
2. Resumption of service delivery, and of access to goods and services
3. Restoration of governance
4. Risk reduction and building back better

Main elements of a recovery strategy

- Recovery vision and guiding principles
- Intended sectoral results
- Priority needs and interventions
- Recovery costs
- Expected results
- Intended outcomes
- Implementation arrangements

Source: Asian Development Bank (Climate Change and Sustainable Development Department).

4 Session 4: The Productive Sector

This session introduces the methodology for assessing the productive sectors, with a focus on examples from the agriculture sector. The step-by-step methodology covers sector team composition and tasks, sources of information, context analysis (baseline), disaster effects, disaster impacts, cross-cutting issues, and recovery and reconstruction needs (Figure 5).

Figure 5: Coverage of Session 4—The Agriculture Sector

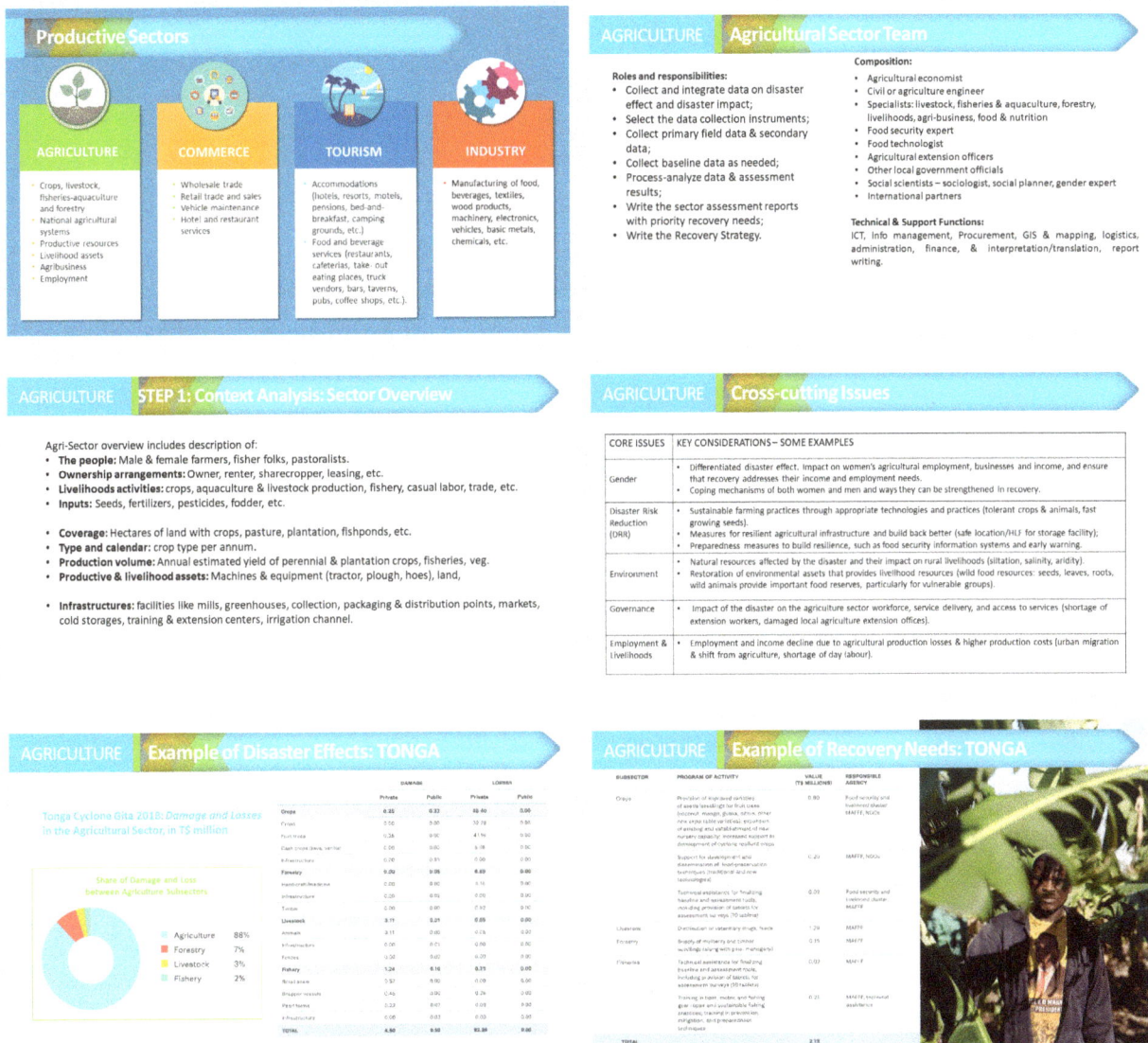

Source: Asian Development Bank (Climate Change and Sustainable Development Department).

5 Session 5: The Social Sector

The session introduces the methodology for assessing the social sector, with examples from the education subsector.

Figure 6: Coverage of Session 5—The Social Sector

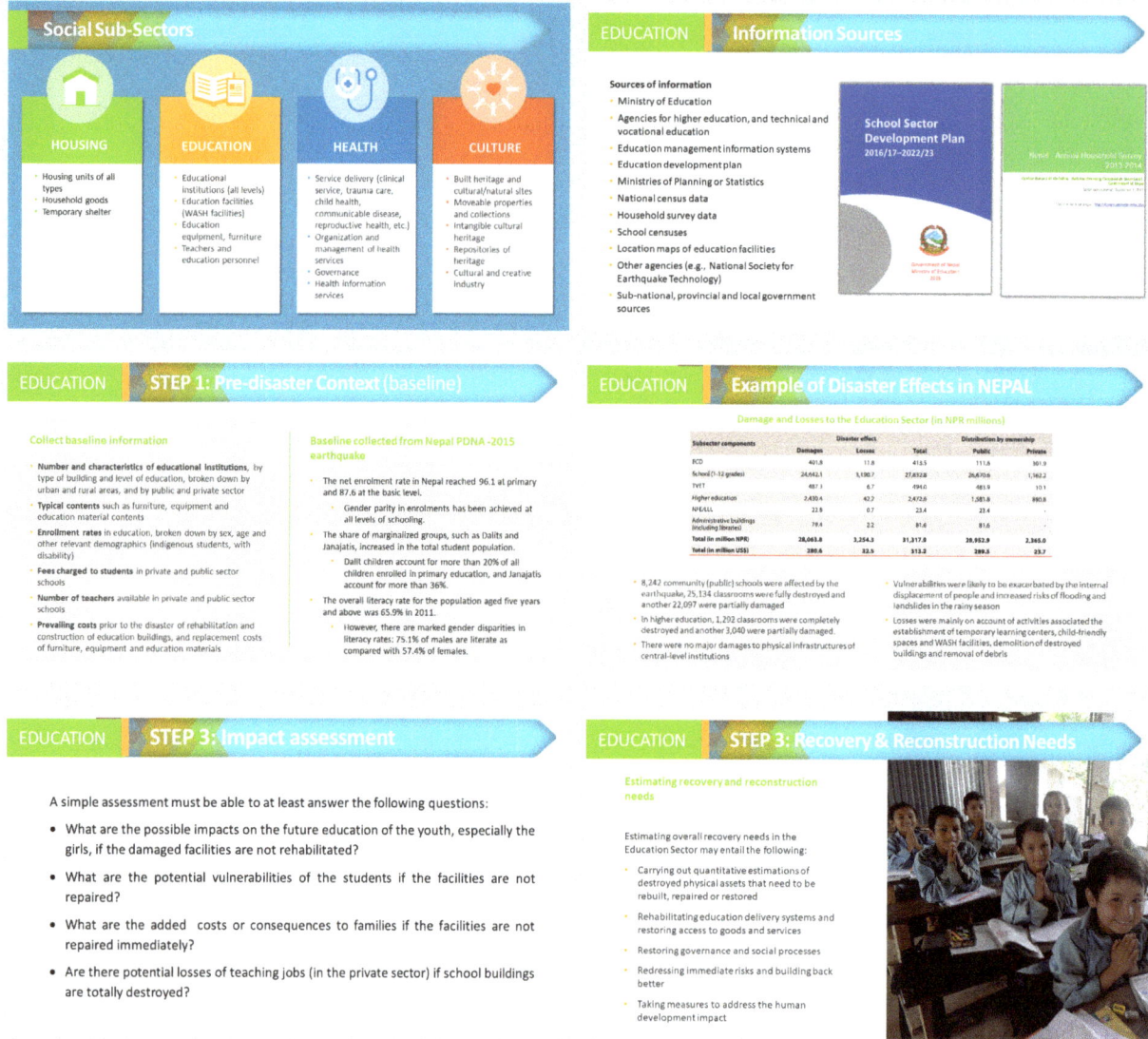

Social Sub-Sectors

HOUSING
- Housing units of all types
- Household goods
- Temporary shelter

EDUCATION
- Educational institutions (all levels)
- Education facilities (WASH facilities)
- Education equipment, furniture
- Teachers and education personnel

HEALTH
- Service delivery (clinical service, trauma care, child health, communicable disease, reproductive health, etc.)
- Organization and management of health services
- Governance
- Health information services

CULTURE
- Built heritage and cultural/natural sites
- Moveable properties and collections
- Intangible cultural heritage
- Repositories of heritage
- Cultural and creative industry

EDUCATION — Information Sources

Sources of information
- Ministry of Education
- Agencies for higher education, and technical and vocational education
- Education management information systems
- Education development plan
- Ministries of Planning or Statistics
- National census data
- Household survey data
- School censuses
- Location maps of education facilities
- Other agencies (e.g., National Society for Earthquake Technology)
- Sub-national, provincial and local government sources

School Sector Development Plan 2016/17–2022/23

EDUCATION — STEP 1: Pre-disaster Context (baseline)

Collect baseline information
- Number and characteristics of educational institutions, by type of building and level of education, broken down by urban and rural areas, and by public and private sector
- Typical contents such as furniture, equipment and education material contents
- Enrollment rates in education, broken down by sex, age and other relevant demographics (indigenous students, with disability)
- Fees charged to students in private and public sector schools
- Number of teachers available in private and public sector schools
- Prevailing costs prior to the disaster of rehabilitation and construction of education buildings, and replacement costs of furniture, equipment and education materials

Baseline collected from Nepal PDNA -2015 earthquake
- The net enrolment rate in Nepal reached 96.1 at primary and 87.6 at the basic level.
  - Gender parity in enrolments has been achieved at all levels of schooling.
- The share of marginalized groups, such as Dalits and Janajatis, increased in the total student population.
  - Dalit children account for more than 20% of all children enrolled in primary education, and Janajatis account for more than 36%.
- The overall literacy rate for the population aged five years and above was 65.9% in 2011.
  - However, there are marked gender disparities in literacy rates: 75.1% of males are literate as compared with 57.4% of females.

EDUCATION — Example of Disaster Effects in NEPAL

Damage and Losses to the Education Sector (in NPR millions)

Subsector components	Disaster effect			Distribution by ownership	
	Damages	Losses	Total	Public	Private
ECD	401.8	11.8	413.5	111.6	301.9
School (1–12 grades)	24,642.1	3,190.7	27,832.8	26,670.6	1,162.2
TVET	487.1	6.7	494.0	483.9	10.1
Higher education	2,430.4	42.2	2,472.6	1,581.8	890.8
NFE&LL	22.9	0.7	23.4	23.4	-
Administrative buildings (including libraries)	79.4	2.2	81.6	81.6	-
Total (in million NPR)	28,063.8	3,254.3	31,317.8	28,952.9	2,365.0
Total (in million US$)	280.6	32.5	313.2	289.5	23.7

- 8,242 community (public) schools were affected by the earthquake, 25,134 classrooms were fully destroyed and another 22,097 were partially damaged.
- In higher education, 1,292 classrooms were completely destroyed and another 3,040 were partially damaged.
- There were no major damages to physical infrastructures of central-level institutions
- Vulnerabilities were likely to be exacerbated by the internal displacement of people and increased risks of flooding and landslides in the rainy season
- Losses were mainly on account of activities associated the establishment of temporary learning centers, child-friendly spaces and WASH facilities, demolition of destroyed buildings and removal of debris

EDUCATION — STEP 3: Impact assessment

A simple assessment must be able to at least answer the following questions:
- What are the possible impacts on the future education of the youth, especially the girls, if the damaged facilities are not rehabilitated?
- What are the potential vulnerabilities of the students if the facilities are not repaired?
- What are the added costs or consequences to families if the facilities are not repaired immediately?
- Are there potential losses of teaching jobs (in the private sector) if school buildings are totally destroyed?

EDUCATION — STEP 3: Recovery & Reconstruction Needs

Estimating recovery and reconstruction needs

Estimating overall recovery needs in the Education Sector may entail the following:
- Carrying out quantitative estimations of destroyed physical assets that need to be rebuilt, repaired or restored
- Rehabilitating education delivery systems and restoring access to goods and services
- Restoring governance and social processes
- Redressing immediate risks and building back better
- Taking measures to address the human development impact

Source: Asian Development Bank (Climate Change and Sustainable Development Department).

6 Session 6: The Infrastructure Sector

The session provides practical insights into assessing the infrastructure sector, with a specific focus on the transport subsector (Figure 7).

Figure 7: Coverage of Session 6—The Infrastructure Sector

Infrastructure Sub-Sectors

TRANSPORT	TELECOMMUNICATIONS	ENERGY	WATER & SANITATION	COMMUNITY
• Road transport • Railroad and air transport • Pipeline transport • Postal services • Transport support, including airports, ports, tunnels, bridges, etc.	• Wired, wireless, satellite telecommunication • Programming & broadcasting • Publishing and information services • Movie, television, music production	• Non-renewable energy • Electricity supply • Power utility companies • Renewable energy • Pipelines and refineries	• Water supply • Sanitation • Solid waste management • Drainage • Hydropower • Agricultural water • Hygiene	• Local small-scale infrastructure such as internal community roads, bridges, footpaths • Community, religious centers • Community water supply systems • Micro solar grids

TRANSPORT — Team Composition

Sector Assessment Team
- Civil engineers
- Road/Transport expert
- Transport economist

Transport Sector Team -Myanmar PDNA 2016 floods
- Economic Advisor to the President
- Ministry of Transport and Communications
- ADB, WB

TRANSPORT — STEP 1: Pre-disaster Context (baseline)

Collect baseline information
- Location and capacities of transport systems (road, air, railroad and pipeline transport, and transport support facilities)
- Number and capacities of the vehicular stock available in each of the systems
- Volume of traffic flow
- Most recent origin and destination surveys in the affected and nearby areas
- Marginal operating costs in each of the transport modes for different types of vehicles
- Annual reports of performance of (private or public) enterprises

Baseline collected from Myanmar PDNA -2016 floods
- 40% of Myanmar's population (20 million people) live in villages without access to all season roads. This isolation limits access to markets, employment, health and education services.
- Myanmar's public road network comprises 157,059 km across 14 states, with only 22% paved.
- The rail network consists of 5,934 km of tracks
- There are 3 international airports, and 30 domestic airports.

Transport mode	Freight (million ton-km)	Passengers (million passenger-km)
Road	88.7	59.9
Railway	4.8	13.5
River	8.0	1.3
Air	Negligible	2.2

TRANSPORT — Examples of Disaster Effects: MYANMAR

Disaster effects in transport sector in Myanmar, in MK million

Subsectors	Damage (in MK million)			Losses (in MK Million)			Total effects (in MK million)		
	Sub-total	Public	Private	Sub-total	Public	Private	Effects	Public	Private
Road	69,823	69,741	82	8,433		8,433	78,256	69,741	8,515
Rail	6,302	6,302	-	80	80	-	6,382	6,382	-
River	50	-	50				50	-	50
Total	76,175	76,043	132	8,513	80	8,433	84,688	76,123	8,565
Yangon	258	258	-	-	-	-	258	258	-

- DAMAGE to roads resulted from inundated pavements and washouts of bridges and culverts.
- 32 key highway links were temporarily severed in 7 states
- Railway line embankments were also severely eroded by floodwaters.
- Bridge piers, abutments, approaches, and superstructures were destroyed by high water levels on floodplains

- LOSSES captured the higher user costs associated with detours and poor condition of roads, as well as the lost profit on the affected Myanmar Railway lines.
- Losses for roads were calculated by considering the additional vehicle operating costs across 16 key highway links assuming these costs were borne by private vehicle operators.
- Calculations included costs resulting from the extra distance required to follow detours during initial closure, as well as marginal costs due rougher road condition on the original route

Impact assessment: Transport

The assessment team of the sector must answer the following questions:

1. What are the **possible effects** on the productivity, government services, on the people, etc. if transportation services are not restored immediately?
2. Will people be able to **access** health and educational services?
3. Will there be **hardships and increased dangers** in commuting for people with disabilities, women, children and the elderly, etc.?
4. Are there **added transportation costs** to families if they will have to travel using alternative routes?
5. Will food supply be affected if transport services are not restored immediately? What will be the **potential impacts to vulnerable groups** (women, children, elderly, etc.) if food supply will be affected?
6. Are there **expected reductions in employment** (whether temporary or permanent) if transportation services are not restored immediately?

TRANSPORT — STEP 3: Recovery & Reconstruction

Estimating Recovery Needs
- Estimated as a direct function of change in economic flow (losses)
- Examples:
  - Opening the traffic in landslide-blocked and washed-out sections of the road
  - Repair of damages such as clearing landslide debris, clearing drains, filling potholes
  - Work relating to monsoon preparedness

Estimating Reconstruction Needs
- Estimated as a direct function of damage
- Examples:
  - Reconstruction of damaged roads, bridges, ports and airports
  - Hydraulic study and revision of design
  - Development of strategic road sub-networks
  - Integration of "build back better" principles in reconstruction

Source: Asian Development Bank (Climate Change and Sustainable Development Department).

As a conclusion to Day 1, the training facilitator will invite participants to share key learnings and reflections. Following this, the facilitator will provide a briefing on the PDNA simulation exercise, presenting the PDNA implementation process along with highlights of each step. Participants are encouraged to dress casually and be prepared for a serious yet enjoyable exercise for Day 2 (Figure 8).

SIMULATION EXERCISE

The simulation exercise is scheduled for Day 2 of the PDNA Introductory Training. The objective is to equip ADB resident mission staff to effectively participate to a PDNA by enhancing their understanding of the methodology and refining practical skills. The following sections provide additional details for preparing and conducting the simulation exercise in Day 2.

CLOSING

At the conclusion of Day 2, participants will be invited to share their insights and reflections. Additionally, the training facilitator will also request them to submit their feedback and comments online. The closing remarks can be delivered by the resident mission country director or representative.

Figure 8: Summary of the Post-Disaster Needs Assessment Implementation Process

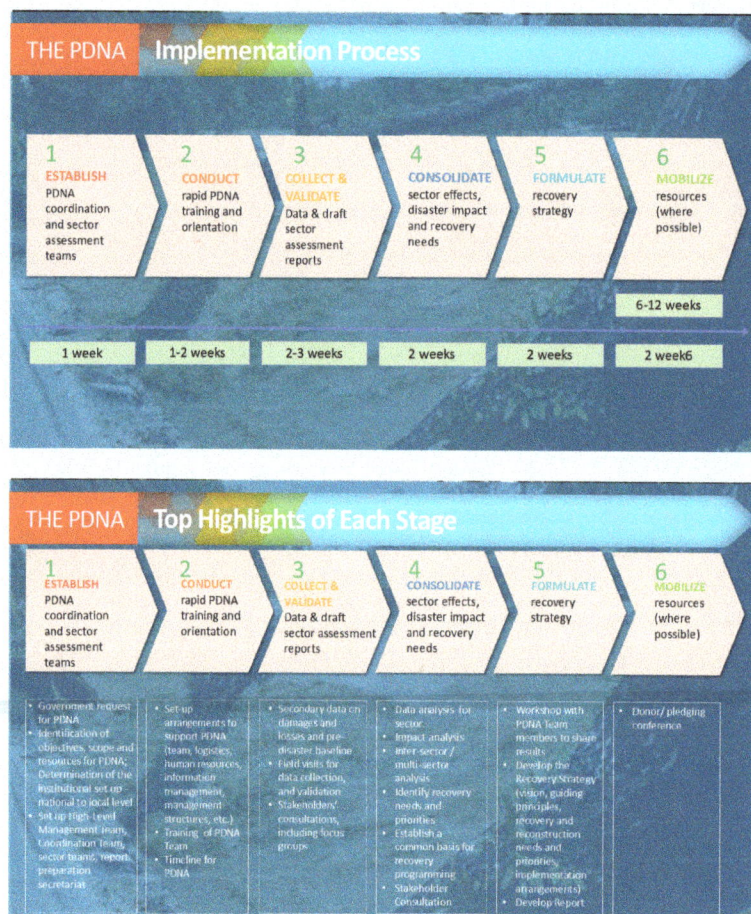

PDNA = post-disaster needs assessment.
Source: Asian Development Bank (Climate Change and Sustainable Development Department).

FURTHER RESOURCES

The following ADB materials are available for participants' reference:

ADB. 2023. Post-Disaster Needs Assessment Introductory Course. PowerPoint presentation. Unpublished. Available upon request.

ADB. 2023. _Disaster Recovery Planning: Explanatory Note and Case Study_. Manila.

ADB. 2022. _Asia Pacific Disaster Response Fund: Second Window: Disaster Recovery Expert Pool User Guide_. Unpublished.

ADB. 2022. _Four Tips for Processing ADB's Emergency Assistance_. Video presentation. Unpublished.

ADB 2021. _Post-Disaster Needs Assessment Overview for ADB Staff_. Unpublished. Manila.

Other key training and materials are also available online:

World Bank Open Learning Campus. _Post-Disaster Needs Assessment (PDNA) Online Training_.

European Commission, United Nations Development Group, and World Bank. 2013. _Post-Disaster Needs Assessment Guidelines Volume A_.

European Commission, United Nations Development Group, and World Bank. 2013. _Post-Disaster Needs Assessment Guidelines Volume B_.

In preparation for the immersive PDNA training experience, careful consideration is given to the training environment and roles of the training team to maximize learning and engagement. These preparations, combined with the designated roles of the training team, ensure a seamless and enriching training experience for all participants.

LAYOUT OF THE TRAINING HALL

It is advisable to conduct the training at an external venue to draw undivided attention from the participants. A training hall of no less than approximately 50–60 square meters works well for a group of about 25–30 participants. The registration desk, beverage and water counters, and food counters should be placed just outside the training hall—close enough for the convenience of participants but with enough buffer to minimize any disruption or disturbance to participants and the activities.

1 Day 1

The recommended layout of the training hall for Day 1 is "banquet style", with 5–6 round tables, each with 5–6 chairs, allowing for a total seating capacity of approximately 30 participants. Additionally, a separate rectangular table is recommended at the back of the room for the training team, including facilitators and co-facilitators.

Post-Disaster Needs Assessment Introductory Training, Sri Lanka Resident Mission, Colombo. Banquet layout of the training hall for day 1 (photo by Thitiphon Sinsupan, Asian Disaster Preparedness Center).

Post-Disaster Needs Assessment Introductory Training, Dhaka. Staff from the Bangladesh and Nepal resident missions attend a day 2 session with an open U-shape layout of the training hall (photo by Anne Orquiza, ADB).

2 Day 2

The recommended layout of the training hall for Day 2 is an open "U-shape," providing ample space inside the group for participants to move around and interact with others during the role play exercise. A small table may be placed in the center of the "U" for microphones and other necessary equipment. The rectangular table at the back of the room for the training team should be retained.

Stationery and Props

Ensure the following stationery and props are ready for the role play (Appendix 1):

(i) Name badges and lanyards: Prepare these for easy identification of participants.

(ii) Overhead projector: This is essential for visual presentations.

(iii) Roving microphones: Have three roving microphones available for audience engagement and questions.

(iv) Lapel microphone: Ensure the session lead has a lapel microphone for clear communication.

(v) Role cards: Cut out the role cards and attach double-sided tape on the reverse for easy sticking on the name badge and use during the simulation exercise. (Appendix 2.)

(vi) Flip charts: Provide three flip charts with stands for visual aids and note-taking.

(vii) Permanent markers: Have a variety of permanent markers (mixed colors) available for writing and drawing.

(viii) Props for the role play: Gather scarf, jacket, necktie, bed sheet, briefcase, handbag, hat or cap, etc., to serve as props to enhance the realism of role-play scenarios.

By having these stationary items and props ready, the facilitator can ensure a smooth and engaging training experience for participants.

FACILITATING THE SIMULATION EXERCISE

To successfully conduct the simulation exercise ("simex"), several functions need to be performed by the training team members. These functions can be assigned to two or more persons from the training team based on the human resources available. At the minimum, the training team may consist of three people, which has a minimum level of redundancy in case of any exigencies. At least one of the trainers should be female to ensure meaningful gender representation and sensitivity in the delivery. Ideally, all the training team members should be adept on the technical content and have experience on simulation exercises, either in delivering it or as a participant to allow for shadowing.

(i) The team leader (Training Lead) will be responsible for delivering the technical presentations, and facilitating the training program and group discussions during the simulation exercise.

(ii) The second member (Simex Facilitator) should have a good understanding of how things typically pan out in a post-disaster scenario, manage the simulation exercise, and participate in the delivery of technical presentations.

(iii) The third member (Training Coordinator) will coordinate the seamless delivery of the training including coordination and logistics and participate in the delivery of technical presentations.

The functions to be performed during the training and their recommended distribution are shown in the Table.

Representatives from the host resident mission (preferably the country director) should be requested to either open or close the training.

Table: Key Training Functions and Recommended Actor

Function	Recommended Actor
Overall training facilitation	Training Lead
Delivery of technical sessions on post-disaster needs assessment fundamentals and recovery planning (sectoral expertise/experience recommended)	All
Facilitation of damage and loss assessment exercise in sectoral groups	Training Co-Lead
Facilitation of role play or simulation exercise	Training Lead and Co-Lead
Facilitation of group reflections, takeaways	Technical Lead
Coordination and logistics	Training Coordinator
Role play in the simulation exercise	Training Lead, Training Coordinator

Source: Asian Development Bank (Climate Change and Sustainable Development Department).

The training participants will engage in a practical learning experience through the simulation exercise. The simulation exercise has been designed to align with the various stages of PDNA, as illustrated in Figure 9. By referring to this visual guide, participants will plan their possible actions for each PDNA stage based on the given disaster scenario.

Figure 9: Highlights of Each Stage of the Post-Disaster Needs Assessment Introductory Training Module

1. ESTABLISH PDNA coordination and sector assessment teams	2. CONDUCT rapid PDNA training and orientation	3. COLLECT AND VALIDATE data and draft sector assessment reports	4. COLLECT sector effects, disaster impact, and recovery needs	5. FORMULATE recovery strategy	6. MOBILIZE resources (where possible)
1 week	1–2 week	2–3 week	2 week	2 week	2 week
• Request by government to conduct PDNA • Identify objectives, scope, and resources for PDNA • Determine the institutional set-up at local to national levels • Set up high-level management team, coordination team, sector teams, and report preparation secretariat	• Set up arrangements to support PDNA (team, logistics, human resources, information management, management structures, etc.) • Train the PDNA team • Set timeline for PDNA	• Gather secondary data on damage and losses and predisaster baseline • Conduct field visits for data collection and validation • Conduct stakeholders' consultations, including focus group discussions	• Analyze data per sector • Analyze impact per sector • Conduct intersector and/or multisector analysis • Identify recovery needs and priorities • Establish a common basis for recovery programming • Conduct stakeholder consultation	• Conduct workshop with PDNA team members to share results • Develop the recovery strategy (vision, guiding principles, recovery and reconstruction needs and priorities, implementation arrangements) • Develop the report	• Conduct donor and/or pledging conference

PDNA = post-disaster needs assessment.
Note: Total duration of PDNA is 6–12 weeks.
Source: Asian Development Bank (Climate Change and Sustainable Development Department).

SIMULATION EXERCISE AGENDA

The detailed agenda of the simulation exercise is outlined in Box 2.

Box 2: Day 2. Proposed Program on Post-Disaster Needs Assessment Introductory Training – Simulation Exercise

Time	Session
DAY 2	
9:30–9:45 a.m.	**Recap of Day 1**
9:45–11:15 a.m.	**Introduction to the Simulation Exercise and Understanding of Stakeholders Involved in PDNA**
11:15–11:30 a.m.	**Break**
11:30 a.m.–1:00 p.m.	Undertaking the Simulation Exercise on Delivering a PDNA Stage I: Pre-Activation and Activation (30 minutes) Stage II: Preparing a PDNA (30 minutes) Stage III: Data Collection and Validation (30 minutes)
1:00–2:00 p.m.	**Lunch**

2:00–3:15 p.m.	Undertaking the Simulation Exercise on Delivering a PDNA (continued)
	
	Stage IV: Consolidation and Analysis (60 minutes)
	    (i) Estimating Damage and Loss (45 minutes)
	    (ii) Identifying Impacts, Recovery Needs and Priorities (15 minutes)
	Stage V: Finalizing Recovery Strategy (15 minutes)

3:15–3:30 p.m.	**Break**
3:30–4:15 p.m.	**Reflections and Observations**
4:15–4:30 p.m.	**Closing**

PDNA = post-disaster needs assessment.
Note: Timings may be modified to suit the country context.
Source: Asian Development Bank (Climate Change and Sustainable Development Department).

FACILITATORS' GUIDE

The scenario-based simulation exercise is designed around a fictional post-disaster scenario at the provincial level. Participants will navigate this scenario by referencing the four PDNA stages.

1 Beginning of the Day

The session builds on the lessons of the previous day and lends a solid foundation for the participants to co-create an immersive learning experience for the benefit of the group.

The facilitator opens the conversation with a recap of the previous day. Participants are invited to take turns and share any reflection or key highlights from the previous day that stayed with them. This conversation often touches upon the differential impact of disasters on various groups within the community and provides a basis for the moderated discussion on roles, opportunities, and limitations of different stakeholders in a post-disaster scenario based on participants' first-hand experience of a disaster event.

The facilitator asks the participants about their first-hand experience of a disaster event and leads the conversation along the following questions:

(i) How were you impacted by the disaster event?

(ii) Who else (or which other stakeholders) did you get a chance to observe closely during the event? What were their main concerns? How did these concerns change with time?

The facilitator concludes the session with a slide on the stages of the PDNA process (Figure 9), to summarize the lessons from Day 1 and introduce the simulation exercise.

2 Introduction to the Simulation Exercise

Moving into the simulation exercise, the facilitator informs that the exercise is based on a fictional post-disaster scenario to help the group understand all the stages of a typical PDNA process by applying the lessons from Day 1. This will help the participants appreciate the various nuances of the event from different vantage points—both quantitatively and qualitatively, to pave the way for a holistic perspective to help the affected people recover from the disaster event with a "build back better" approach. The facilitator invites all the participants to engage fully with the exercise and contribute to each other's learning.

3 Warming Up

Preparation: Role cards for the simulation exercise (Appendix 2) are to be displayed on the table in the center of the "U."

The facilitator introduces the exercise as a shared process to gain a deeper understanding of the effects and impacts of a disaster. The facilitator then invites the participants to choose any of the personas for the simulation exercise by selecting a role card displayed on the table.

The personas represent typical roles required for a PDNA exercise—from activation to development of recovery strategy. These include a clear grouping consisting of the following:

(i) community members especially vulnerable sectors such as elderly, differently abled, indigenous peoples, children, and women);

(ii) local government agencies that often serve as the front-line functionaries;

(iii) national and subnational government PDNA agencies, which, depending on the scale of the disaster, may be led by various heads of subnational and national government departments;

(iv) donor community, e.g., current and potential development partners who may assist the government with the recovery efforts; and

(v) other actors such as nongovernment organizations, academia, and media.

A detailed list of the roles to be played is in Appendix 1.

4 Getting into the Role Play

After participants have chosen a persona, the facilitator invites them to spend 15 minutes going through the disaster scenario and dwell on the following questions:

(i) What is the role of this persona in PDNA?

(ii) What are the agenda associated with this persona or role?

(iii) What are the challenges and limitations of the persona or role?

(iv) What are your thoughts to creatively develop your role as the PDNA simulation is played out?

The exercise will be interrupted by the Training Coordinator posing as a news reader to read out the scenario below:

BREAKING NEWS:

Good [morning/afternoon/evening], I'm [Your Name], and this is a breaking news update from Gyanapradesh.

We are on the ground, revisiting the aftermath of Cyclone Jalagiri that struck this region with ferocity on 22 July 2020.

Cyclone Jalagiri developed from a low-pressure system over the Bay of Bengal and made a devastating landfall in Suryapura Province within a span of 24 hours. Wind speeds reached a staggering 75–85 kilometers per hour, leaving a trail of destruction in its wake.

The impact was swift and severe. Five provinces are grappling with extensive wind damage, flooding, and landslides. Transportation, agriculture, and utilities are crippled, leading authorities to issue urgent evacuations in vulnerable areas, particularly in coastal areas.

As of this moment, the weather in Gyanapradesh is calm, but the scars of Cyclone Jalagiri are still visible. The affected provinces are now in the midst of recovery and rehabilitation, a daunting task considering the widespread devastation. The toll on human life and infrastructure has been catastrophic. Heavy rainfall caused flash floods and landslides, resulting in the tragic loss of 53 lives, with 98 still missing, and 538 injured needing urgent medical attention.

The human cost is immeasurable, and the entire community is grappling with the aftermath of this disaster. Emergency services remain on high alert as residents are urged to stay vigilant. The unpredictability of our environment is a stark reminder of the challenges we face.

We'll keep you updated as the situation develops.

Reporting live from Gyanapradesh, I'm [Your Name]. Back to you in the studio."

At this point, the simulation exercise facilitator commences the role play by handing out the scenario sheets to all the participants (Handout 1).

Typhoon Ketsana (Ondoy) dropped 455 mm (17.9 in) of rain on Metro Manila in a span of 24 hours on 26 September 2009. A month's worth of rainfall washed away homes and flooded large areas in a single day, killing hundreds and stranding thousands in the city and nearby provinces. (photo by ADB).

Handout 1: Disaster Scenario—Gyanapradesh

BACKGROUND

Gyanapradesh is a small coastal island with a range of hilly areas and several large rivers that flow into the coastal delta. With 15 provinces and a total population of 7.2 million, Gyanapradesh includes a diverse set of ethnic groups with varying levels of socioeconomic development. The coastal areas are generally more developed than the inland areas, which have significantly lower average household income. The disaster risk profile of Gyanapradesh includes annual exposure to cyclones and storm surges in the coastal areas; and riverine floods, landslides, and forest fire in the inland hilly areas.

On 22 July 2020, Gyanapradesh was hit by a category 3 cyclone (based on Saffir-Simpson scale). A low pressure area had formed over the Bay of Bengal that over the next 2 days developed into a cyclonic storm named "Jalagiri." Cyclone Jalagiri gradually approached the island and made landfall around 10:30 a.m. on 23 July 2022. The cyclone crossed the island coast through Suryapura Province with a wind speed of 178–208 kilometers per hour (kph) and gusts of up to 115 kph. It moved westward and emerged into the Gulf of Mannar, affecting five provinces and causing wind damage, flooding, and landslides in the eastern, central, and northwestern parts of the island along with associated disruptions to transport, agriculture, and utilities, among others.

Authorities evacuated the people living in vulnerable coastal and low-lying areas to safe locations, and all schools in the five provinces were closed for a week. Relief camps were set up in schools and response activities were coordinated with the police and armed forces. Eastern sea areas were rough and naval and fishing activities were abandoned in the eastern sea and adjoining areas.

Cyclone Jalagiri brought heavy rainfall that caused flash floods and landslides resulting in damage and losses to infrastructure and other sectors in five provinces. In the aftermath, 53 people were confirmed dead, 98 missing, and 538 with injuries requiring medical treatment. The Gyanapradesh government decided to conduct a post-disaster needs assessment (PDNA) for each affected province. Your team has been assigned to conduct the assessment in Suryapura Province.

PROFILE OF SURYAPURA PROVINCE

The geography of Suryapura Province is a thin stretch of 2,500 square kilometers of land from the coastal to inland hilly areas. Tables H1.1, H1.2, and H1.3 present selected socioeconomic information on Suryapura.

Table H1.1: Demography of Suryapura Province

Human Development Indicators	Value		
Poverty incidence	30% of households		
Prevalence of malnutrition	10%		
Maternal mortality ratio	10/10,000		
Infant mortality rate	20 per 10,000 live births		
Demography	**Male**	**Female**	**Total**
Total population	80,000	70,000	150,000
Total number of those below 5 years old	10,000	15,000	25,000
Total number of those above 60 years old	30,000	35,000	65,000
Total number of differently-abled	1,300	1,200	2,500
Household Description	**Male**	**Female**	**Total**
Average size	3	2	5
Average number of children per family	2	1	3
Total Number of Families or Households	**% of Total**	**Total Number**	
Total number of households		30,000	
Headed by males	90%	27,000	
Headed by females	10%	3,000	
With sanitary toilets		29,000	
Without sanitary toilets		1,000	
With electricity		25,000	
Without electricity		5,000	
Belonging to ethnic minority group		5,000	

Source:

Table H1.2: Sources of Income in Suryapura Province

Main Sources of Income	Number of Households	Average Monthly Income ($)	Average Value of Household Assets ($)	Number of People	
				Male	Female
Self-employed					
Farming	15,000	100	200		
Fishing	5,000	100	150		
Livestock	1,000	90	200		
Poultry	1,000	80	200		
Microenterprises	1,000	70	200		
Trading (shops and stores)	3,000	120	300		
Services	1,000	100	200		
Transport workers	500	130	300		
Employed					
Daily wage laborers	1,000	150	400		
Skilled workers (mining)	300	250	600		
Professionals	5,000	500	5,000		
Others					
Other sources					
Pension	1,000	100	600		
Outside remittance	50	200	500		

Source:

Relief goods for the victims of Typhoon Ulysses. Volunteers from nearby towns help unload relief packs and sacks of rice to be distributed to the victims of Typhoon Ulysses in Rodriguez, Rizal, on November 29, 2020 (photo by ADB).

Table H1.3: Social Services in Suryapura Province

Public Basic Services	Quantity	Total Capacity (persons)	Power Source		Source of Potable Water Supply				
			Electricity	Others	Type 1	Type 2	Type 3	Type 4	Type 5
Primary School	5	500	X			X			
High School	3	3,000	X						X
University	1	2,000	X						X
Health Centers	5	250	X						X
Hospitals	1	500	X						X
Province Hall	1	200							X
Fire station	1	50	X						X
Police station	1	50	X						X

Notes:

Capacity of basic services refers to enrollment in schools and the number of patients per day in medical facilities.

For water supply source:

Type 1 is sourced from a spring.

Type 2 is individual well with hand pump.

Type 3 is shared community well.

Type 4 is community faucet.

Type 5 is piped-in faucet.

Source:

ROLE PLAY—DELIVERING A POST-DISASTER NEEDS ASSESSMENT

The Simex Facilitator displays the chronology or stage of the PDNA exercise to get the role play into motion. Upon announcement of the stage of PDNA, relevant personas are invited to come up front. Others who do not have a role in the stage of the PDNA serve as observers.

The Facilitator allows the personas involved in the stage to plan the role play for that stage. Then the role play for the stage at hand is carried out in the time allotted as shown in Table H1.4.

Table H1.4: Role Play for A Post-Disaster Needs Assessment

PDNA Stage	Activity	Time	Output
Stage I: Pre-activation and activation	Role play	30 minutes	PDNA teams identified
Stage II: Preparing a PDNA	Role play	30 minutes	PDNA plan (area, timeline, sectors) prepared; all stakeholders trained
Stage III: Data collection and validation	Role play	30 minutes	Qualitative understanding of baseline information gathered, sectoral data, collected, and data validated
Stage IV: Consolidation and analysis	Group work	60 minutes	Quantitative damage and losses for the given sectors assessed; impacts identified; priorities for recovery needs articulated; and intersectoral linkages for comprehensive recovery planning identified
Stage V: Finalizing recovery strategy	Role play	15 minutes	PDNA findings presented; recovery vision and strategy agreed upon

Source:

Handout 2: Exercise on Estimating Sector Disaster Effects, Impacts, and Needs

The exercise on assessing disaster effects, impacts, and needs as detailed in this Handout will enable the participants to determine and estimate the damage and losses based on the given scenario. Participants will be regrouped to work on the sector assigned to them, review the pre- and post-disaster information, and identify potential impacts on the economy and the people affected by the disaster. This will enable them to list types of programs, activities, and projects for the recovery of the sector.

Working in respective sector groups, participants will review the pre- and post-disaster information and complete the following tasks for three sectors, namely, agriculture, transport, and housing:

(i)   Estimate the damage and losses.

(ii) Based on the socioeconomic baseline information of Suryapura Province and the damage and losses, identify potential impacts on the economy and the people who were affected by the disaster.

(iii) Based on the impact assessment, identify qualitatively the types of activities and/or projects needed for the recovery of the sector (It is not necessary to quantify the amounts.)

(iv) Given that the initial budget for the entire recovery is limited, identify the top three priority activities and/or projects for the sector.

(v)   Present sector results to the group.

SCENARIO: AGRICULTURE SECTOR (AGRICULTURE, LIVESTOCK, FISHERIES, AND FORESTRY)

Damage

For agriculture, damage is related to the following costs:

- Repair of partially damaged assets and/or
- Replacement of totally destroyed assets and infrastructure, such as

  » **Structures or buildings.** Includes storage, animal shelters, irrigation, research laboratories, and other structures.

  » **Equipment and other machinery.** These are various instruments used for agriculture purposes like tractors, mechanical harvesters, farm tools, other important assets, etc.

  » **Agriculture products, inputs, materials, and supplies.** These are stocks normally kept by farmers such as harvested rice, corn, seed stocks, fertilizers, pesticides, veterinary medicines, etc.

  » **Plantations fully destroyed (uprooted).** The totally destroyed standing crops and/or plantations like palm oil, coconuts, tea, mangos, etc. are considered agricultural assets and are valued at their replacement costs (replanting and maintenance cost until again in full production). A negative effect on production is considered a loss and accounted for under "losses" until the crops are fully productive again.

Losses

Losses may stretch even beyond the year that the disaster occurred. It is expressed in monetary value at current prices. Losses in the agriculture sector include the following:

- **Loss or reduction in production or income.** The reduction of income will occur when planted crops, livestock, fisheries, forestry, etc., are partially damaged by disasters. This can be estimated by considering the pre-disaster expected income less post-disaster expected income. Totally destroyed seasonal crops like rice, corn, and vegetables that are ready to be harvested are valued at farm gate prices.

- **Reduction in future production or income.** Long-term income losses from harvests can be due to factors such as the following:

  » **Degradation of land by floods, landslides, prolonged droughts, etc.** This will happen if agricultural lands are rendered less productive after a disaster, which can extend years after a disaster. This can be estimated by considering the pre-disaster expected income less post-disaster expected income spread through the years until the production levels normalize.

  » **Loss of production on account of totally destroyed standing crops and trees.** This can be estimated by considering the pre-disaster expected income spread through the years until the standing crops and trees are productive again to the same level.

- **Investment losses.** In agriculture, an important type of loss is the investment loss of farmers when the standing crops are destroyed by a disaster. If these happen and the farmers (or growers) are not able to replant within the year, the value of investment put into the destroyed crops will be considered as a loss. Otherwise, losses are estimated as the value of the reduction of the expected production.

- **Higher or added production cost.** The total cost of production in the year will increase if the farmers replant in time to harvest within the year. This will mean that the farmers (or growers) will incur a higher production cost to produce the same volume of harvest within the year. The added cost of production will be considered a loss by the farmers (or growers).

- **Additional expenses to clean up the debris of destruction, retrieval of buried assets, etc.**

Baseline Information

(i) Agricultural crops are mostly rice, maize, and vegetables.

(ii) There is one commercial tea plantation that employs 100 people as tea pickers.

(iii) Livestock and poultry are mostly backyard in nature.

(iv) One irrigation canal is used for farming in the province.

(v) Suryapura Province supplies 30% of the rice in Gyanapradesh.

Table H2.1: Crops and Forestry in Suryapura Province

Subsector	Area Planted (ha)	Crop Cycle per Year	Average Yield (MT/ha)	Farm Gate Price ($/MT)	Investment Cost per Hectare per Stage of Growth ($/ha)		
					Newly Planted	Middle Stage	Mature
Crops							
Rice	2,000	2	4	300	240	420	720
Maize	1,000	1	5	250	300	540	900
Vegetables	500	3	3	120	50	100	200
Others							
	Area Planted						
Permanent Crops	**Size (ha)**	**Yield (MT/ha/year)**	**Price ($/MT)**		**Newly Planted**	**Middle Stage**	**Mature**
Tea	500	10	500		20	500	1,000
Others							
	Area Planted						
Forestry	**Size (ha)**	**Yield (MT/ha/year)**	**Price ($/MT)**		**Newly Planted**	**Middle Stage**	**Mature**
Timber					1,000	5,000	10,000
Others							

ha = hectare, MT = metric ton.

Source:

Table H2.2: Fisheries in Suryapura Province

Subsector	Farm Gate Price ($/MT)	Average Value of Production ($/year)
Marine Fisheries		60,000
Inland Fisheries		
Assets	**Average Replacement Cost ($)**	**Average Repair Cost ($)**
Boats	5,000	500
Engines	500	100
Nets	200	50
Traps and Cages	100	30
Gears	200	50
Others		

MT = metric ton.

Source:

Table H2.3: Livestock and Poultry in Suryapura Province

Assets (Livestock)	Number (heads)			Average Value ($/head)			Average Value of Production per Year ($)
	Young	Juvenile	Mature	Young	Juvenile	Mature	
Buffalo				120	350	1,000	300,000
Cow				80	160	800	400,000
Sheep				30	70	120	150,000
Goat				20	50	100	150,000
Others							
Poultry							
Chicken				1	2	3	10,000
Ducks				1	2	3	20,000
Others							

Source:

Based on the field visit, the following were noted:

(i) 800 hectares of middle-stage rice were affected. It is estimated that production per hectare of the affected rice farms will be reduced by 20% in 2020 because of the cyclone.

(ii) 100 tons of harvested maize were totally destroyed.

(iii) 300 hectares of newly planted vegetables were totally washed away by the floods and could be replanted, entailing higher investment costs.

(iv) 50 hectares of tea plantation were uprooted and need to be replanted. It should take 3 years until the new plants can be productive again to the same level.

(v) 2,000 mature chickens and 500 ducks were declared to be missing and presumed dead.

(vi) Veterinary medicines worth $5,000 and pesticides worth $3,000 were destroyed.

(vii) 15 fishing boats were partially damaged.

(viii) Marine fishing production is expected to be lower by 20% for the year.

Table H2.4: Estimating Damages and Losses for the Agriculture Sector in Suryapura Province

Description	Year 1		Year 2	Year 3	Total		Remarks
	Damages ($)	Losses ($)	Losses ($)	Losses ($)	Damages ($)	Losses ($)	
Total							

Source:

SCENARIO: TRANSPORT SECTOR (LAND, WATER, AIR, AND RAIL TRANSPORT)

Damage

In the transportation sector, the damage is related to the cost of the following:

- Repair of partially damaged assets and/or
- Replacement of totally destroyed assets and infrastructure such as the following:

  » **For land transport.** This includes all types of roads, bridges, and allied structures like culverts, drains, shoulders, as well as all types of land vehicles that are part of the land transportation system, buildings, and equipment.

  » **For water transport.** This includes ports, jetties, inland waterways, ferries, and other assets.

  » **For air transport.** This includes airports, aircraft, buildings, and equipment.

  » **For railroads.** These include trains, railway tracks, buildings, and equipment.

  » **Materials and supplies and other equipment.** These include computers, tools, books, furniture, etc.

Damage in the transport sector will occur at the time of or shortly after the disaster although some damage may become obvious only after a longer period. Damage is measured in physical terms (such as kilometers of roads, number of structures, number of equipment) for which the monetary value of repair or replacement is subsequently estimated at current prices.

Losses

Losses are the values of foregone revenues or income due to the change in economic flows (income and expenditures) during the period of recovery and reconstruction following the disaster. They are the current value of goods and services that were not and/or will not be available over a time span due to the disaster until full recovery is attained. In the transport sector, losses include the following:

- urgent expenditures to re-establish traffic flows after transport assets have been affected like the cost of temporary bailey-type bridges, removing of debris, cleaning of drains, detours, etc.;
- higher cost of transport due to the use of alternative, longer, and lower-quality roads over the recovery and reconstruction period;
- losses in revenue of the enterprises—both public and private—that operate the transport services like bus companies, airlines, shipping lines, trains, airports and ports, among others;
- cost of dredging river channels to enable vessels to dock; and
- other unexpected expenditures that may arise due to the disaster like clearing of debris.

Losses will take place during the entire period of recovery and reconstruction of the sector and may stretch even beyond the year that the disaster occurred. It is expressed in monetary value at current prices.

Baseline Information

(i)   There are various types of roads and bridges in Suryapura Province.

(ii) The airport is also located in Suryapura Province and services passengers going to other countries, including foreign tourists.

Table H2.5: Roads and Bridges in Suryapura Province

Type of Road	Total Length by Classification (km)					Average Replace-ment Cost ($/km)	Average Repair Cost ($/km)	Average Number of Users per Month	
	Exp.	NH	SH	MDR	Rural			Persons	Vehicles
Concrete	70					350,000	200,000	300,000	100,000
Asphalt		100				250,000	150,000	200,000	50,000
Bituminous			100			200,000	100,000	50,000	10,000
Graveled				50		100,000	50,000	20,000	1,000
Earth									

Type of Bridge	Number by Classification					Replace-ment Cost ($/m)	Average Repair Cost ($/m)	Average Number of Users per Month	
	Exp.	NH	SH	MDR	Rural			Persons	Vehicles
Steel	5					50,000	3,000	300,000	100,000
Concrete	15					20,000	1,000	200,000	50,000
Wood		20				5,000	200	50,000	10,000
Others									

Exp. = express road or bridge, km = kilometer, m = meter, MDR = major province road or bridge, NH = national highway or bridge, SH = state highway or bridge.
Note: "Rural" means rural or other road or bridge.
Source:

Based on the field visit, the following were noted:

(i) The following roads and bridges were damaged:

   a) 15 kilometers (km) of asphalt roads in national highways

   b) 10 km of graveled roads in major district roads

   c) 5-meter long steel bridge on express road is totally damaged

   d) 10 meters of a concrete bridge on express road is partially damaged

(ii) The roofs of two public bus terminals were blown off by strong winds, requiring $5,000 each for repair.

(iii) Ten buses from a private bus company were submerged in flood waters, requiring $2,000 each for repair.

(iv) 200 private cars were damaged, requiring a total of $100,000 to repair them all.

(v) Because of the damage to the buses, roads and bridges, the private bus company is expected to lose $20,000 for 2 months.

(vi) The runaway of the airport was full of debris, which will cost $10,000 to clear.

(vii) Runway lights were submerged in flood waters, which will need $50,000 to repair.

(viii) The airport will be closed for 2 weeks, which is expected to reduce the airport's income by $10,000 per day.

(ix) About 10 km of railroad tracks were damaged, requiring $2,000,000 worth of repairs. It will take 1 month to repair the track, which will amount to $100,000 in revenue losses.

Table H2.6: Estimating Damage and Losses for Transport Sector

Description	Damage ($)		Losses ($)		Total		Remarks
	Public	Private	Public	Private	Public	Private	
Total							

SCENARIO: HOUSING SECTOR

Damage

In the housing sector, damage is valued as the cost of the following:

- Repair of partially damaged houses and other related assets

- Replacement of totally destroyed houses and other related assets

Physical assets related to all types of dwellings or housing facilities include structures (housing units), premises (garages, fences), common areas and facilities (elevators, generators, gardens, swimming pools), and the contents inside the individual dwellings or houses such as furniture, appliances, and other valuables (like antiques, books, computers, etc.).

Damage is measured in physical terms for which the monetary repair or replacement value is subsequently estimated.

Losses

Losses are the values of foregone revenues or income due to the change in economic flows (income and expenditures) during the period of recovery and reconstruction following the disaster. They are the current value of goods and services that were not and/or will not be available over a time span due to the disaster until full recovery is attained.

Losses in the housing sector include

- foregone income from housing rents, fees and other related sources of income, which will last until the housing units are repaired;

- cost of unforeseen expenditures like temporary shelters, equipment, etc. to be used while the housing units are under repair or reconstruction; and

- costs involved in the demolition or removal of debris, etc.

Losses will take place during the entire period of recovery and reconstruction of the sector and may stretch even beyond the year that the disaster occurred. It is expressed in monetary value at current prices.

The cost of repair or replacement that will be borne by the individual owners of the housing units will be part of the private losses. On the other hand, if the cost of temporary shelters, removal of debris, etc. will be shouldered by the government, their total value should be considered as public in nature. It is assumed that the assets in the housing sector are of private ownership.

Baseline Information

(i)   There are 30,000 households in Suryapura Province.

(ii)   Most of the families living in the rural areas are farmers with type 1, type 2, type 3, and type 4 housing.

Table H2.7: Types of Housing in Suryapura Province

Housing Classification		Number of Houses	Ownership (%)		Number of Houses for Rent	Average Number of Occupants	
Types	Description		Male	Female		Female	Male
Type 1	Grass and/or bamboo	8,000	99	1	0	3	3
Type 2	Mud	4,000	99	1	100	2	3
Type 3	Wood	5,000	90	10	100	2	3
Type 4	Stone	3,000	90	10	200	2	2
Type 5	Metal and/or asbestos sheets	1,500	80	20	100	2	2
Type 6	Brick	2,500	80	20	100	2	2
Type 7	Concrete	5,000	70	30	200	1	2
Type 8	Others	1,000	70	30	100	1	2
Total							

Source:

Table H2.8: Average Value of Contents, Rent Per Month, Replacement Cost and Average Repair Cost for Different Types of Housing in Suryapura Province

Particulars	Values of Various Types of Housing ($)							
	Type 1	Type 2	Type 3	Type 4	Type 5	Type 6	Type 7	Type 8
Average value of contents	500	1,000	3,000	7,000	10,000	12,000	15,000	20,000
Average rent per month		50	100	250	300	400	500	600
Average replacement cost	2,000	3,000	5,000	10,000	15,000	17,000	40,000	50,000
Average repair cost	200	300	500	800	1,000	2,000	5,000	7,000

Note: The following are the types of dwellings:

Type 1: Grass and/or bamboo

Type 2: Mud

Type 3: Wood

Type 4: Stone

Type 5: Metal and/or asbestos sheets

Type 6: Brick

Type 7: Concrete

Type 8: Others

Source:

Based on the field visit, the following were noted:

(i) A total of 3,000 type 1 houses; 500 type 2 houses; and 1,000 type 3 houses were totally destroyed. The contents of these houses were also totally destroyed.

(ii) A total of 300 type 4 houses, 200 type 5 houses, 100 type 6 houses, and 50 type 7 houses were partially damaged. No house contents were damaged.

    c) Of the partially damaged type 4 houses, 50 are for rent and will require 1 month for repair before they can be rented out again.

    d) Of the type 7 houses, 20 that were partially damaged are for rent and will require 2 months for repair before they can be rented out again.

(iii) There is no damage to type 8 houses but the total cost of clearing the debris within their premises will amount to $50,000 altogether.

(iv) All of the households that lost their houses and 50% of households whose houses were partially damaged in the disaster were provided temporary shelters for a period of 6 months on private land. The rent for private land was fixed at $30,000 for this period. The cost of temporary shelters per household is $500.

(v) Habitat services such as water and sanitation, electricity, and solid waste management were agreed at $50,000 per month for all families.

Table H2.9: Estimating Damage and Losses for Housing Sector

Description	Number of Houses Damaged		Damage ($)	Losses ($)	Total ($)	Remarks
	Partial	Fully				
Total						

Source:

Reflections and Observations

Following the role play, the simulation exercise facilitator guides a discussion centered around feedback and key learnings with the participants. The following questions may serve as a ready reference for the simulation exercise facilitator to lead the discussion:

i) What is the one key message or reflection that has stuck with you?

ii) How has this training enhanced your understanding of ADB's role in post-disaster recovery?

This crucial step allows everyone to reflect on their experience, share their observations, and delve deeper into the insights gained from the training and simulation exercise. By facilitating this discussion, the simulation exercise facilitator creates a supportive environment where participants can openly express their thoughts, enabling a comprehensive understanding of the training outcomes and fostering a collaborative learning atmosphere within the group.

Appendix 1: Role Play

Persona	Pre-activation and Activation (Establish PDNA Coordination and Sector Assessment Teams) Week 1	Preparation of PDNA (Training and Orientation, PDNA Plan) Week 1	Data Collection and Validation Weeks 2–3	Consolidation and Analysis (Sector Effects, Impacts, and Recovery Needs) Week 4	Formulation of Recovery Strategy Weeks 5–6
Sector Specific Grouping					
Representative from Disaster Management Center, Authority, or Department	X	X	X		X
Representative from Ministry of Agriculture, Housing, or Transport	X	X	X	X	X
Director and/or Representative from Road Development, Housing, or Transport Authority		X	X	X	X
Representative of a leading nongovernment organization (social sector expert)		X	X	X	
Representative from the Asian Development Bank (economist)	X	X	X	X	X
Representative from United Nations Development Program or World Bank (Engineer)	X	X	X	X	X
Responders at Field Location					
Director of Suryapura Provincial Road Development, Housing, or Transport Authority		X	X	X	
Provincial secretary of Suryapura		X	X	X	
Village development officer			X		
Village head			X		

continued on next page

Table *continued*

Persona	Pre-activation and Activation (Establish PDNA Coordination and Sector Assessment Teams)	Preparation of PDNA (Training and Orientation, PDNA Plan)	Data Collection and Validation	Consolidation and Analysis (Sector Effects, Impacts, and Recovery Needs)	Formulation of Recovery Strategy
	Week 1	Week 1	Weeks 2–3	Week 4	Weeks 5–6
Disaster-affected farmer (man) who lost three brothers and his father in the event, and whose small rice farm has been rendered uncultivable due to a huge deposit of sediments and salinity			X		
Disaster-affected fisherman who lost five laborers working with him, and whose boat has been damaged and his fishing gear lost			X		
80-year-old woman who has lost her son to the disaster			X		
Private bus company, which has two of its six buses partially damaged by the disaster			X		
Disaster-affected man with a family of seven whose poultry farm and meat shop have been completely destroyed			X		
Disaster-affected single woman whose house has been destroyed and whose children could not go to school			X		
Representative of media			X		

PDNA = post-disaster needs assessment.
Source:

Appendix 2: Role Cards

Secretary, Ministry of Disaster Management	Representative, Department of Disaster Management
Representative, Ministry of Finance	Representative, Ministry of Agriculture
Representative, Ministry of Housing	Representative, Ministry of Transport
Representative, National Bureau of Statistics/Planning	Director, Suryapura Provincial Road Development Authority
Representative (Economist) Asian Development Bank	Representative (Engineer) United Nations
Director of a Leading Nongovernment Organization (Social Sector Expert)	Village Development Officer
Provincial Secretary, Suryapura	Representative, Road Development Authority
Village Head	Owner of a Private Bus Company
Disaster-Affected Farmer (male)	Disaster-Affected Fisherman
Disaster-Affected Single Woman	80-Year-Old Woman
Economist	Social Sector Expert
Engineer	Media

Typhoon Haiyan (Yolanda) Damage and Rehabilitation. Houses destroyed by Typhoon Haiyan in Palo, Leyte (photo by ADB).